Samuel McChord Crothers

Interpreter of Life

By
Frederick M. Eliot

1930
The Beacon Press, Inc.
Boston, Massachusetts

Designed by GRANT RITCHIE

Printed in the United States of America

The substance of the following pages was given in the form of an address, at the service of dedication of a tablet in memory of Mr. Crothers, in Unity Church, St. Paul, Minnesota, Sunday, December 8, 1929.

SAMUEL McCHORD CROTHERS

Interpreter of Life

O N AN AUGUST Sunday morning in the year 1886, a young minister stood before a small congregation in the city of St. Paul, Minnesota, to preach a trial sermon. He was twenty-nine years old, though he looked nearer nineteen; and in spite of his diffident manner he already had behind him ten years of experience as a preacher in Kansas, Nevada, California, and Vermont. As he faced this new congregation in Minnesota, the thought of his earlier adventures in so wide a range of churches must have helped to give him confidence.

He needed all the confidence he could muster, for this congregation had high standards by which to judge his efforts. Fourteen years before, a group of men and women, most of whom had been brought up in eastern Unitarian churches, had decided that there ought to be a church of that denomination in St. Paul; and, with characteristic determination, they had proceeded to carry out their purpose. They had already had three ministers, of whom one had stayed for seven years and had left upon the young society an indelible impression; and the young candidate must have realized that his fitness for the pastorate of Unity Church would be largely determined by comparison with this one among his predecessors.

It would be difficult to imagine a greater contrast than that between William Gannett and Samuel Crothers. One of them had been born in Massachusetts, the other in Illinois. One had been educated at Harvard, the other at Princeton. One represented, by birth and nurture, the finest traditions of Boston Unitarianism; the other was a child of Scotch Presbyterian stock, reared on the Westminster Shorter Catechism, and imbued, from his earliest days, with the doctrines of John Calvin and Jonathan Edwards. From the point of view of a Unitarian church, William Gannett had been born to the purple. His father had been the colleague and successor of the great William Ellery Channing, of the Federal Street Church; and if the younger Gan-

nett had broken away from the family tradition
both in his more radical thought and in his de-
cision to go west, he none the less belonged in
the very innermost circle of New England Unitarianism. Samuel Crothers, on the other hand,
had come out of the Presbyterian fellowship
only a few short years before; his standing
among the Unitarians was still questionable.

Gannett was a rebel and a poet. Crothers
was neither. The process by which he had
outgrown the theology of his Presbyterian
ancestry and birthright had had nothing
violent about it, nothing sudden or revolu-
tionary, and his imaginative power, greater
than Gannett's, lay in another field than that
of poetry. Almost the only thing the two men
had in common was a passionate desire to make
religion a reality in the lives of their fellow-men.

Aware of this divergence of gifts and experience, what sort of sermon could the "come-
outer" preach, to win the sympathy of a
congregation so recently under the powerful
influence of a "born and bred" Unitarian? We
know very little about it, for Mr. Crothers never

{7}

used a manuscript after his student days, and
he left behind him no notes for this particular
sermon. We do know that it was a success, for
it led to a call that was accepted and that in-
augurated a seven-year pastorate. But of the
sermon itself we have only a single paragraph,
happily preserved by the church chronicler. Yet
that paragraph is enough to explain why he re-
ceived the call, and those of us who knew him
in the days of his maturest power as a preacher
can detect, in its sentences, the ring of conviction and the daring reach of thought that
made him one of the great teachers of religion
in our time.

> "What foundation have you for a
> belief in God and Immortality? I
> have none; but what need is there
> for a foundation? The earth is not
> sustained by a foundation, but is im-
> pelled through space."

Surely nobody listening to those words could
doubt for a moment that the man who spoke
them belonged in the pulpit of a free church.
The chrysalis of orthodoxy had been wholly
left behind, and a free mind was testing its

wings for flight toward new and more significant truths. If this man was a "come-outer," he had most certainly come the entire distance. Yet there was nothing disillusioned or despairing about his radical words, nothing suggestive of the pale negations of liberalism. His mind was free, yet plainly constructive; daring in its intellectual venture, yet courageous and confident. Is it to be wondered at that the St. Paul Unitarians called him, or that they still take pride in the fact that he accepted their call? During the years of his ministry among them, they watched his mind develop and his powers of utterance grow from week to week, and when he left them to become minister of the First Parish in Cambridge, they continued to watch his career, convinced that all his greatness was but the natural outgrowth of the young-hearted preaching they had known and loved in St. Paul.

The world knew Mr. Crothers chiefly as a lecturer and essayist, and it isn't strange that his reputation as a preacher should have been thus overshadowed. He could never have been a "popular" preacher in any period, and the times in which he lived were peculiarly unfavorable for really first-rate preaching. He knew nothing of the "art of homiletics" and would have scorned to practice it, had he known it. The tricks that sometimes, even today, fill a church with people who enjoy listening to a series of anecdotes strung on a slender chain of mildly religious argument, would have seemed intolerably cheap to him. He took for granted that the members of his congregation had brought their minds to church with them, and that they wanted to use them as actively as he used his. Careless listeners got little from his sermons, and casual visitors, who heard him only once, were apt to go away unimpressed. But those who heard him Sunday after Sunday, through the years, came to regard him as a preacher of amazing power. They would willingly let all the essays slip away into oblivion, if that were the necessary price to pay for keeping the picture of his gentle figure standing in the high white pulpit of his Cambridge church, with the light of spiritual knowledge and passion shining through his eyes, and for hearing the voice that, on so many occasions, uttered, what were for them, the words of eternal life.

The secret of any great preacher's power is as elusive as the secret of personality. Essentially, I suppose, the two secrets are the same, for a great preacher must be a great personality. But method has much to do with it, also, and method can be more easily analyzed. The students at the Harvard Divinity School used to be told by their instructors to "go and hear Crothers preach, but never, under any circumstances, try to preach the way he does." The warning was salutary, for many a young theologian began his career as a slavish, though usually unconscious, imitator of the minister of the old First Parish across Harvard Square. Some of us took years to get over the habit, for we imitated even the intonations of his voice. But in a more fundamental sense, I think the advice was bad, for the method of preaching Mr. Crothers used is the only one that is likely to be fruitful when one is preaching to modern-minded people. It may not attract the crowd, but it will attract educated men and women, and it will feed their souls—provided the man who uses it is a preacher of genuine native ability.

The heart of his method was the habit of taking his hearers into his confidence. They knew, from the opening sentence, that he was going to be entirely candid with them, and that is the very first condition of effective preaching nowadays—though it is a more difficult condition to meet than most laymen realize. Mr. Crothers accomplished it by the way in which he approached any subject with which he dealt. "Here is a problem," he would seem to say by his manner of starting to preach, "here is a problem that interests me, and that, I think, is important for anyone who is trying to be both honest and religious in his thinking. Let me tell you just what the problem is, as I see it; and then let me tell you the results of my own thinking about it thus far. I am not at all sure that I have the answer, but at any rate this is the general direction in which I believe it will be worth while searching. Perhaps by talking it over together we can get a little closer to the truth."

For those who wanted to be told what to believe, such preaching was, of course, wholly unsatisfactory. None of the dogmatists, whether conservative or radical, could get much from such sermons. But for those who looked upon religion as a quest, this frank acceptance of the "university point of view" in religious thinking was most reassuring. It broke down, at the outset, the barriers of artificial authority that still often hedge about the preacher. It was a public repudiation of the whole set of ideas that have made the pulpit often called a "coward's castle." Here was a religious teacher to whom a thoughtful, independent-minded man could listen, without compromise or mental reservation. Here was a preacher who claimed nothing for himself, except that he was telling, with perfect candor, what seemed to him true and important things about life, as he had found it.

As he talked, he seemed like one of the characters in Bunyan's *Pilgrim's Progress*—a book which he knew almost by heart, and from which he used to quote almost every time he spoke. After Christian has been led astray by Mr. Worldly-Wiseman, and brought back to his true pilgrimage by Evangelist, he is told to stop at the Interpreter's House, where he will be shown many excellent things. Christian follows this counsel, and is entertained by the Interpreter, with genuine cordiality. His host takes him into the "significant rooms" in his house, and tells him the meaning of what he sees; after which, Christian goes on his way, enlightened and encouraged.

Well, Mr. Crothers was just that kind of Interpreter, and every time we heard him preach, we felt as though we had been in the Interpreter's House. He knew how to make us feel at home with him, and he knew how to show us significant rooms in his house by the pilgrim way, so that we too could go on with fresh courage and assurance. The hospitality of his mind was freely given to anyone who had the wit to seek it, and those who entered the doors which he held open for them, found, within his dwelling, an interpretation of life that restored their souls.

To serve men, in that fashion, requires very special gifts and the widest possible range of human experience. The Interpreter must know life in all its aspects, and his heart must instinctively comprehend all sorts and conditions of men. He must have travelled far and wide through the kingdoms of the earth, and in imagination he must have lived in every land and in every age. And then he must have, in supreme degree, the skill that will enable him to bring to each individual in need the refreshment, the wisdom, which his own experience has brought to him. Such Interpreters appear but seldom among men, and Mr. Crothers was one of them. Let us look together at a few of the significant rooms in his house, into which he has taken us, and from which we have come forth, renewed in spirit.

Over the door of one of the larger rooms on the ground floor appeared the legend "Geography—chiefly American." The room was filled with pictures, maps, and miniature

models of all sorts, collected from all over the
world, and assembled without any apparent
system or purpose. As you looked at them,
you suddenly became aware of the fact that
there was magic in this room, for the various
objects moved about and fitted into one another
in a most extraordinary way. The maps, espec-
ially, were alive with motion and gave you the
impression that you were not so much looking
down at them as actually standing in the places
indicated upon them. Mountains, plains,
rivers, hamlets, cities—instead of being marks
upon the paper, they were all, for the moment,
as real as you were, and each scene, as you
looked at it, made you feel as though you had
lived in that particular spot all your life. You
felt at home in each place, and yet you were
always conscious of the existence of all the
rest of the world. Your view was parochial
and planetary, at the same time.

After you had gazed for a while at the maps
and objects in the room itself, the Interpreter
took you to a window that looked out over the
surrounding country. It was his American win-

dow, and, as you looked out, you beheld a con-
stantly changing panorama of American life.
The same magical quality that belonged to the
contents of the room was found in the view
from the window. At every moment you felt as
though you were standing in the very center of
what you were looking at. Each individual scene
was as vivid as though you were actually a part
of it, and yet you never lost the sense of the
continental sweep of America, as a whole. And
the magic had the further effect of giving you a
sense of history as well as of spatial extension.
The past was as living as the present.

At one moment you were in a mining-camp
high up among the peaks of the Rockies; at the
next, you were on the plains of Nebraska, with
the great sweep of an unbroken horizon en-
circling the vast fields of wheat and corn; then,
with disconcerting abruptness, you were climbing
a stony New Hampshire hillside, looking down
upon a little village, with green and white houses,
and a lovely church spire rising from beside the
common. In one flashing instant you saw the
early settlers on Cape Cod, toiling and wor-

shipping, yet finding life a much more delightful experience than you had ever supposed those rather grim Puritans and Separatists knew enough to appreciate; then it was the indomitable migration of the Mormons across the central prairies, until they reached the freedom and promise of their new home in Utah; and then it was the little homesteads of Illinois and Iowa and the Dakotas—little only in the apparent insignificance of any one household amid the vast extent of the fertile plains, but great in the implications of what human skill and courage could achieve. And all of it was America—that was the constant background of everything you saw—all of it America, and all of it yours, because you belonged to America, and because all of America belonged to you.

Very quietly, the Interpreter stood beside you at the window and looked with you at the ever-changing views. "It's interesting, isn't it?" he would say. "Interesting to see how many different kinds of places we Americans live in, and in how many different ways we have worked and endured and conquered. Have you, by any chance, the habit of noticing the names of the stations you pass on the railroad, and wondering how they happened to be there? It's a most entertaining and rewarding habit, I assure you. Take, for example, the various places named Bethlehem. Finding out why this name is scattered all over the country opens up a fascinating chapter in our history. I wonder how many of the workers in the steel mills in Bethlehem, Pennsylvania, ever heard of Count Zinzendorf? You know, there's much more religion in the background of our American life than most of us ever realize, and it's rather a pity that we overlook it. Somebody could write a charming book about the spiritual significance of the names of American towns. Why don't you write it?"

I remember well the last sermon I heard Mr. Crothers preach. He had just come back from Utah and a trip through Zion National Park, and he was full of enthusiasm over its beauty and grandeur. He told us how he had been struck by the names given to the various masses of rock that constitute the most impressive features of that desert region—such names as "The Temple," "The Great White Throne," "The Altar of Sacrifice." At first, he had been puzzled to find biblical names attached to such strange freaks of nature; but then he remembered that the religion which produced the Bible had come out of the deserts of Syria and Arabia and Mesopotamia. And so the sermon became a study of the influence of the desert—of great, open, barren stretches—upon the soul of man, and of the perennial need to renew our sense of contact with this source of spiritual insight. The cool white meeting-house was transmuted that morning into a room in the Interpreter's House, from which we journeyed into far places where the human spirit first came to a knowledge of its kinship with eternal realities.

Beyond the Geography Room was another of equal size labelled "American Idealism." This room also was full of surprises. As you crossed its threshold, the first thing to catch your attention was a model of the Roosevelt Dam, so ingenious and perfect that it seemed as though only the builder of the dam could have made it. The Interpreter would smile at your astonishment, as though he knew that you were saying to yourself, "I had no idea he was interested in engineering"; and then he would begin to talk about the dam. "That is a symbol of our American concern with material things, and at the same time a symbol of the often neglected fact that there is nothing in all the world more truly idealistic. Do you remember Carl Sandburg's poem about the engineers, 'There are no bars across the way'? Here in America, we propose to master everything, and use everything as we master it for the attainment of our own purposes and ideals. We *know* we can conquer the forces of nature, and we *believe* we can also conquer the forces of human nature. We intend to create a 'dirigible civilization,' and that is the most exalted dream the world has ever seen."

Everywhere in that room you saw America at work, and everywhere you suddenly began to see the idealism behind the struggle. The idealism of the doctors, of the social workers, of the teachers, of the farmers, of the miners, of the business men, of all Americans, even when they supposed they were only concerned with the mad scramble for the almighty dollar—under the spell of the Interpreter's comment you saw it all very clearly, and believed in it with sudden, passionate conviction.

And then, sometimes, the Interpreter's mood would change, and he would point out to you, with blazing indignation, the places where men were betraying their heritage of idealism. I shall never forget the day he took me to see "The Birth of a Nation," and the white heat of his anger at what seemed to him an outrageous denial of the ordinary rights of his fellow-citizens of Negro descent. He spoke once, at a public meeting in Boston, in protest against the denial of the right of free public discussion of birth control and the Ku Klux Klan. He had no sympathy with either movement, but he deeply resented the attempt to deprive them of their rights. American idealism, as he saw it and taught us to see it, was too big a thing to descend to petty or prejudiced tactics. It was as broad as the Great Plains and as lofty as the Sierras.

You had to climb a long flight of stairs before you came to the room over the door of which was inscribed "Members of One Body." The moment you entered it, you knew you were in a church, but what kind of church it was you could never finally decide. Sometimes it seemed as unadorned as a Wee Free kirk or a Quaker meeting-house, sometimes it was filled with the incense of a Roman Catholic cathedral. The windows were sometimes ablaze with the glories of Chartres, and then it would seem as though the colors were merely the gorgeous hues of a sunset, or of autumn foliage seen through the plain glass of a Puritan church. It was all very puzzling at first, but after a while you began to understand what the Interpreter was trying to make you see and feel.

As he talked with you about the history of religion, all your prejudices slipped away. He made you see the sincerity—sometimes, to be sure, the sad sincerity—of every search for religious consolation and power. He revealed to you the truth in every formulation of religious belief, no matter how crude or dogmatic or presumptuous. He understood, and in a measure taught you to understand, all the passion for truth and righteousness that lies behind the labels we use so glibly and often so stupidly—Catholic, Calvinist, Methodist, Mystic, Rationalist, yes, even Atheist. He had been a good listener to them all; and though he always had his own personal convictions, he never lost his ability to hear the authentic voice of religion speaking in the strangest of her many dialects. "Members of One Body" he called them, and so he always thought of them.

There were no limits to his understanding—none at all. He had nothing of the easy tolerance that ignores differences, until they reach the point of really meaning something, and then abruptly draws the line. He saw all the differences very clearly, and always refused to minimize them; but he rejoiced in their presence, and delighted in their persistence. He drew all the lines required by straight thinking, and drew them definitely; but his understanding heart knew no lines whatever. This natural largeness of heart was instantly recognized by all who met him. He was welcome everywhere, and listened to with respect by all. Very likely the tale is apocryphal, but it is none the less characteristic, that once, in Salt Lake City, he found himself sitting in the place reserved for the high officials of the great Mormon Tabernacle. He would have felt at home there, and the authorities of the church would not have been scandalized to have him in their midst. They might have asked him questions, as he undoubtedly would have asked questions of them; and there would have been profitable conversation and learning on both sides. At any rate, it is true that he sat on the platform with "Billy" Sunday in Boston, once, and smiled with amusement when "Billy" berated the Unitarians. The next Sunday, he preached about "Billy," with such sympathy that some of his Unitarian hearers were shocked. His text on that occasion was "And David danced before the Lord, with all his might."

Many other rooms there were in that amazing house, but we must be content with a few words about only one more. It was high up, near the top of the house, where the sounds of the busy street were almost lost. When you went in, the place for its label was empty of any lettering; but when you came out, and glanced back at the closing door, you saw upon it your own name.

Inside that room, you talked with the Interpreter about a great many different things, and sometimes it took a long while for you to discover what the real topic of conversation had been. Perhaps it was not till an hour or two later, when you had left the house, that you realized why your name had appeared so surprisingly upon the door of that upper room. Then it became clear, and you understood what the Interpreter had been doing while he talked to you ostensibly about quite indifferent matters. Very gently, very amusingly, but very thoroughly, he had been showing you your self— your follies and frailties and sins, and also your powers and possibilities and dreams. The precious assortment of grievances, with which you had entered, had been revealed to you for what they really amounted to. The spirit of whining complaint against an unkind fate had somehow been dragged up from its lurking-place in the dark, and the light had cured it for very shame's sake. Some magic had unmasked all the timid doubts which you had allowed to assume the disguise of sane and sensible reasons, and you beheld them in their true colors of sheer cowardice. You saw yourself as the Interpreter saw you. You saw your relation to the world as he saw it. And you were humbly grateful to him for what he had opened your eyes to see. "Your soul has been empty all the time, and you did not know it; you thought it was the universe that was empty."

Searching though the rebuke may have been, it never stirred you to self-defense or to resentment against the Interpreter. What he said was so plainly true, and so plainly kind in its intent. Nor did he ever send you away discouraged. He had so high an estimate of what you might become, so much confidence in your power to do

what you ought to do, that you came away
filled with determination to justify his faith. If
he believed in you, how could you help believ-
ing in yourself? If he had found the world a
good place in which to live, and life itself an
infinitely varied and delightful experience,
somehow you could not admit that you found
them anything less. "Rectitude—serenity—joy;
and the greatest of these is joy." With those
words ringing in your ears, how could you
maintain your "defeatist" philosophy?

Perhaps you tried to resist—for a few min-
utes. And then you saw him looking at you, a
little shocked and a good deal amused by your
stubborn folly. And so you laughed at yourself, and went along, and tried again.

Bliss Perry once said of Mr. Crothers' essays
that they "mount to Paradise by the stairway of
surprise," and the words are equally applicable
to his sermons. I doubt whether he ever
preached without surprising at least some of his
hearers, and I am sure that the surprise always
lifted them higher than they had been before.
The unexpected flash of spiritual insight invari-

ably lighted up a happier truth than they could have anticipated; and gradually they learned, by the example of his way of teaching, to share his basic conviction that what is today unknown will make tomorrow a happier and a better day. He would have subscribed, with all his mind and with all his soul, to the lines of William Gannett:

"Our faiths are foolish by falling below,
Not coming above, what God will show."

He loved the great texts, in the sacred scriptures, that exult in the vision of unexpected good to come. "Beloved, now are we the sons of God, and it doth not yet appear what we shall be." "Eye hath not seen, ear hath not heard, nor the heart of man conceived, the things that God hath prepared for them that love him." "The morning stars sang together, and all the sons of God shouted for joy."

This eager sense of expectancy may have come, in part, from his evangelical heritage, as the intimate knowledge of the Bible surely did; but his was very far from the traditional Christian confidence in the coming of the Kingdom of God. His spirit had ceased altogether to be dependent upon the guarantees and certainties of man-made theologies. He put no trust in human efforts to map out the course of events and diagram the route to the heavenly places. His was a far deeper trust than that, for it was trust in the process itself, in the growing wonder and beauty of creative experience.

He felt himself part of a mighty enterprise, so vast in its scope and so tremendous in its all-inclusive sweep, that all our human efforts to bring it within the bounds of a neat little system of thought were patently absurd; and yet, because he felt himself part of it all, because he felt at home in the world, he dared to trust what he could not hope to understand.

There was an immortal child in his heart, as there is in the heart of every poet and seer. When he wrote a prayer for the children of his Sunday School, he put this sentence into it: "May we live in the world as in Thy great house." That reminds one of what Francis Thompson said about Shelley: "It is the child's power of make-believe raised to the nth power"; and it also carries an echo of the saying of the teacher of Galilee: "In my Father's house are many mansions."

He loved the mansions of this earth, for he had found them filled with joy and delight. How could he help looking forward to the mansions he had not yet explored, with the keenest anticipation? Always, here or elsewhere, it would be his Father's house. "So long as the creative process, with all its surprises, goes on," he once said, "so long will there be that quick recognition through hearts ready to receive, as they daily delight in God's will, and rejoice all the more when it is fulfilled in unexpected ways." What lay ahead of him, he could not imagine. It was certain to be a surprise. And he had discovered that most surprises are happy ones. The final words of the last prayer he spoke in his own pulpit were "blessed surprise."

Only a soul that has kept its child-like quality could face the unknown with such perfect confidence, but it is not enough to keep a quality with which one is born. Something must be wrought out by one's own experience and added to one's birthright. The rectitude and serenity and joy with which Mr. Crothers faced life were those of a soul that has won freedom for itself—a soul utterly free, yet mature and wise in its liberty. I wish some one of his old friends might have gone to him in the days of his ripest powers of mind and heart, and asked him his own question of the early St. Paul sermon. "What foundation have you for a belief in God and Immortality?" Without the slightest hesitation, I believe he would have given the same answer: "I have none." But then he would have gone on to say, with his disarming and reassuring smile, "But what need is there for a foundation? The earth is not sustained by a foundation, but is impelled through space."

What need has a free spirit for a solid rock on which to stand, when it has wings with which to fly? What need has a full-rigged ship for moorings in some sheltered harbor, when before it lie the perils and glories, the storms and exultations, of the open sea?